Do you have any ideas for subjects which could be included in this exciting and innovative series? Could your company benefit from close involvement with a forthcoming title?

Please write to David Grant Publishing Limited
80 Ridgeway, Pembury, Tunbridge Wells, Kent TN2 4EZ
with your ideas or suggestions

SUPER SELLING With NLP

Forthcoming titles in this series will include

- *Positive PR!*
- *Writing Great Copy!*
- *Win-Win Negotiation!*
- *Coping Under Pressure!*
- *Motivation Skills!*
- *Getting and Keeping a Positive Attitude!*

SUPER SELLING
With NLP

Russell Webster

60 Minutes Success Skills Series

Copyright © David Grant Publishing Limited 1998

First published 1998 by
David Grant Publishing Limited
80 Ridgeway
Pembury
Kent TN2 4EZ
United Kingdom

99 98   10 9 8 7 6 5 4 3 2 1

60 Minutes Success Skills Series is an imprint of
David Grant Publishing Limited

All rights reserved. Except for the quotation of short passages for the purposes of criticism and review, no part of this publication may be reproduced, stored in a retrieval system, or transmitted, in any form or by any means, electronic, mechanical, photocopying, recording or otherwise, without the prior permission of the publisher.

British Library Cataloguing in Publication Data
A CIP record for this book is available from the British Library

ISBN 1-901306-12-7

Cover design: Steve Haynes
Text design: Graham Rich
Production editor: Paul Stringer
Typeset in Futura by
Archetype IT Ltd, web site http://www.archetype-it.com

Printed and bound in Great Britain by
T.J. International, Padstow, Cornwall

This book is printed on acid-free paper

The publishers accept no responsibility for any investment or financial decisions made on the basis of the information in this book. Readers are advised always to consult a qualified financial adviser.

All names mentioned in the text have been changed to protect the identity of the business people involved. Any resemblance to existing companies or people is entirely coincidental.

Contents

Welcome: About *SUPER SELLING*   9

Chapter 1: NLP: An Edge for Life   11
NLP in a nutshell
Diary of a bad sell
Sure-fire openings

Chapter 2: Getting to Know Your Customer   15
Is the key to success the close?
Changing your attitude
Buyer's remorse
Avoiding buyer's remorse
Learn to be honest
Work with and for your customers

Chapter 3: Changing Your Approach   19
Learning to like and be liked
Asking the right questions
Diary of a bad sell 2
Work on your attitude
Gathering intelligence
Before you meet the buyer

Chapter 4: Learning SUSS   27
First impressions count
Starting to SUSS
Looking and feeling the part
State of mind
Golden handshakes
Understudying
Body language
Mind methods

Chapter 5: Seek and Ye Shall Find 41
Seeking the right information
What people want when they buy
Selling benefits, not boxes
The right way to ask questions
Giving Satisfaction
A little about product knowledge

WELCOME

About *SUPER SELLING*

Can you really learn how to be a super salesperson in just one hour? The answer is a resounding "Yes". This book provides you with enough insight into modern sales techniques to enable you to totally revise the way you think about your business and the way you deal with other people.

Is this book for you?

You may already be selling for a living and wanting to increase your commission cheques. You may be about to embark upon a new career in selling or simply wishing to learn how to sell yourself to people or influence them a little more proficiently. The skills we will teach you in this book will never change: you will, simply by becoming better and better at dealing with others.

Super Selling is a collection of hands-on tips and real-life examples to help you become a much more effective sales person. It offers a guide to dip into for ideas and help. And, equally important, by using the skills taught in this book, you will learn to interact much better with other people.

In a world that is changing rapidly so too are selling techniques. *Super Selling* is the smart answer! Don't expect a jargon-filled book, with page after page on 'closing techniques' and 'how to identify buying signals'. That's old hat. What this book will teach you is how to empathise with people and how to get them to like you.

That sounds rather weak and flaccid, doesn't it? Isn't the perfect sales person meant to be aggressive and macho in their techniques? Actually, NO.

In the changing business environment, you need to develop new people skills to be successful. The 'Gordon Gecko' approach to business, which essentially adopts a 'win at any costs' strategy (even if it involves half bludgeoning your customer into a deal), is gone for ever. This book will teach you new skills for a new age.

How to use this book

The message in the 60 Minutes Success Skills Series is 'it's OK to skim'. Each book is written in a way that allows you to flick through and find the help you most need. You do not have to read it all at one go or do everything we advise straight away.

You will find that there are some graphic features used throughout the book to help you extract key information quickly. Basic advice and examples are given as bullet points.

These features ask you to think about something – they set the scene and identify the problems by prompting you to consider familiar attitudes and situations.

With the problems diagnosed, these features give you the framework for an action plan – they will help you to change your behaviour patterns in a positive way.

These features appear at the end of each chapter. They are checklists which summarise all the advice given throughout the chapter and are also a useful reminder of what's where when you come back to look at this book in the future.

As you read through the book, you will come across lots of tips and practical advice on how to make a big impact when selling. You could start by just going straight to any of the boxed features, which will ask you either to think about a problem or to do something about it and give you some ideas.

If you're really pushed for time, you can always go direct to the tips at the end of each chapter.

Good luck!

NLP: An Edge for Life

Chapter 1

What's in this chapter for you

NLP in a nutshell
Diary of a bad sell
Sure-fire openings

NLP in a nutshell

Neuro Linguistic Programming – it sounds very technical and sophisticated. Certainly over the past few years numerous thick books devoted solely to the subject have been published. In a nutshell it is the science of how the brain (neuro) deals with verbal and non-verbal language (linguistic) and the system the brain uses to write and retrieve that language or information (programming).

If that sounds at all complicated then lets simplify it: it is a state-of-the-art communication tool. It is an incredibly powerful mechanism that you can use in all of your dealings with other people and your dealings with yourself: your self-talk. Understanding its applications fully can dramatically improve all of your relationships with other people and also build your self-esteem and self-confidence!

Diary of a bad sell

> Have you ever been in a sales situation, and rapidly realised you have got off to a bad start with a customer – the meeting just got worse? No matter what you try to do, you know that you are not going to succeed. Did you think you might as well just give up?

Let's start this book by looking at a recent experience of mine.

I was in a car showroom whilst my friend was paying for his car being serviced. On the windscreen of a silver car was its price tag – it was very expensive! Below the price the monthly repayments were listed. My mental arithmetic is better than average and it just didn't compute. So I stood there, cogs whirring and scratching my chin for a moment trying to figure it out.

It must have been the chin scratching – for a long time known as a 'buying signal' – because the next thing I know there's a salesperson standing next to me.

"So, are you interested?" he asked.

Quite frankly, I wasn't. And, the way in which he asked me sealed it – even if I had been interested, he was not going to sell it to me. So before he even launched into his sales pitch I was on the defensive. He proceeded to then hamper his cause further.

"It is a lot of car for your money," he said.

"What happens if I don't like big cars?" I thought. I also didn't feel too comfortable about suddenly having to think about parting with my hard-earned money. I stepped back a pace or two. He obviously didn't notice my body language.

"It does nought to sixty in eight and a half seconds!" he continued.

No doubt, he was really intending to impress me further with his sales prowess and knowledge of what I liked in a car. Having neither met me before, nor bothered to find out much about me, he was making a few assumptions based upon his belief of what makes a good car.

Nought to sixty in eight and a half seconds, I thought. How did he know that this was not slower than the car I was currently driving?

"Guess what insurance group it is?" he went on.

I wasn't really in the mood for quiz shows, and I definitely didn't give a damn about which insurance group it was in. "I haven't got a clue," I replied. I really was not warming to this fellow at all.

"Would it surprise you to know that it's only a group fifteen?" came the unwanted reply.

"That's quite interesting," I mumbled, not in the least bit interested.

I think he thought he had me hooked then. He asked me what my current car was, and, having informed him, he swiftly pronounced that I was definitely going to save a fortune and also that the fuel consumption figures were going to impress me. (He knew me very well by this stage.) Then he started going for the kill.

"Doesn't it look great in silver?" he announced.

I really didn't want to get into an argument with him, but I really don't go for silver cars personally. I don't mind other people's silver cars, I just don't want to own one myself. So I changed the subject and asked him how the repayment figures work.

"After the two years' repayments you'd be left with a lump sum payment," he informed me, "whereby you could either pay it off to own it, or use the residual value as a trade-in allowance."

Very neat I thought. Hire it for two years and then have a vehicle that is worth less than you owe on it.

One of my personal values was that I liked to own my cars as quickly as possible.

"What a great way to buy a car, hey?" he enthused.

I quickly used the polite form of 'don't call me, I'll call you', and asked him for his business card. Of course, I thanked him for his help, and then my friend and I left.

He really knew how to *SUSS* out his potential buyers didn't he?!

> **Don't be like my useless car salesman! Don't make assumptions on what you presume other people's values may be.**

On the way back to the car I told my friend Steve that I was actually considering a change of car, and that had the salesman asked a few sensible questions at the outset, created a little rapport with me, sussed me out properly and put me in a more receptive frame of mind then he might have got somewhere with me. Maybe not with that particular car, but as a potential customer for a different car more suitable to my requirements.

> **Can you see the classic errors this salesperson made, especially his opening line which had closed my mind straight away?**

My friend asked me what opening might have made me more receptive. My answer was this: if the salesman had come up to me, with a nice smile on his face and said something like *"Have you been thinking about the possibility of changing cars recently?"* then he would, without threatening me in any way, have opened my mind up into 'possibilities' and 'changing cars' mode and received his first 'Yes' from me.

Had he continued from there and asked me what type of car I was currently driving, what I liked about it and what was important to me personally in a car then he would have been on a much better track.

My experience with the car salesman may well ring true with you – we've all done it in the past, charging in on false assumptions without a hope of getting the sale from the moment we've started.

> Analyse some of your own recent failures (we've all had them!) Why did you not get the sale? Did you make some basic errors, or was the sale not there to be made? If the former, then learn from your experience.

There are always important lessons to be learnt from your mistakes, so don't ignore them. Instead, look at them carefully and try to avoid the same pitfalls in future.

> Tips on the basics
>
> 1. Never assume everyone thinks the same and values the same things.
> 2. Smile when you make your approach
> 3. Don't mention filthy lucre straight away.
> 4. Ask questions and listen to the answers – adapt your pitch according to what you hear, not what you expect to hear.
> 5. Analyse your failures and learn from the experience.

GETTING TO KNOW YOUR CUSTOMER — Chapter 2

What's in this chapter for you

Is the key to success the close?
Changing your attitude
Buyer's remorse
Avoiding buyer's remorse
Learn to be honest
Work with and for your customers

> " When I started my sales career at the age of twenty-one, I really was naive and inexperienced. I had had absolutely no structured training whatsoever. At the end of the first day I was ready to quit, my baptism truly being of fire. The circumstances in which I had to sell were of the primeval sort – ten salesmen lined up like hunters trying to sell a car to some innocent, unsuspecting soldier on the way to do some shopping in his local NAAFI shop in Germany. "
> **– David Prendle, advertising manager**

You can still witness similar types of operation to David's if you go away on holiday to popular sunny holiday resorts – young salespeople lined up by the road side attempting to sell you tickets to something or other, such as go-carting or a time-share viewing.

> " It's all about having balls, as far as I can see. We get paid just to get people into the development, so I go for the timid or gormless looking people and just talk at them. Most say 'yes' just to get rid of me, it seems. And I can't see how my company makes any money out of it; half the people I get don't have the money for time-share. However, I've got to live and my boss seems quite happy. "
> **– Sam Dillon, time-share tout**

To many people, selling remains the domain of the pushy and aggressive personality types. Sharp suited, they get their foot in the door and you will be forced to agree to the vacuum cleaner demo, or the double glazing quote, or whatever, just to get rid of them. And what is it that most of these salespeople want? Nine times out of ten, they're desperate to 'close the sale'

> *After my terrifying and difficult start, I decided to hone my skills and really work at it. I went on a couple of courses, and read some books on selling techniques. Everything pointed to 'closing' the sale.*
>
> **– David Prendle**

JARGON buster

Closing the sale: *In essence, this is the technique and process of actually breaking down the customer until you can write up the order. By the time you reach the end of this book, the term 'closing the sale' will be forever wiped from your memory – hopefully!*

To this day I still hear people talking about a certain 'close' and other special 'closing techniques'. Everyone seems besotted with the order-taking element of the sale and seem to blindly ignore the process that must take place before they can even dream of taking an order.

> *Since those early days, I have sat in on many sales presentations – often with members of my own sales team – and time and time again witnessed this headlong rush to get to the close, quickly trying to overcome objections, like papering over the cracks on the wall. Sometimes it works; more often it doesn't.*
>
> **– David Prendle**

Have you ever been in the situation where, from the moment of entering your environment, the salesperson appears to have nothing else on his or her mind other than closing you into their product. How do you feel when that happens?

There was a time when I used to be totally in awe of those people who could talk the proverbial hind legs off a donkey. You must have come across some of them too; they could sell sand to the Arabs or ice to the Eskimos. What great salespeople they are.

Or are they?

GETTING TO KNOW YOUR CUSTOMER

They may close more sales than most, write up more orders than most, but those sales don't always 'stick'. A sale that sticks stays sold until the product is delivered and paid for.

> There is a sales syndrome called **buyer's remorse** that afflicts many of those people who have been given the hard sell. After the excitement of being sold to is over, the customer realises that he or she has been railroaded or convinced to sign on the dotted line when, actually, they would have liked rather more time to think about it.

Reasons why Buyer's Remorse kicks in

Nowadays, certainly if people are buying or selling expensive goods (cars, electrical goods or home improvements of some sort), there is some kind of credit scheme on offer to finance the purchase. In many countries, written into the credit offer will be a cancellation clause, which gives the customer the right to cancel within fourteen days. A surprising number do – very often for one, if not all, of the following reasons:

- *it was not actually the product that they wanted*
- *they could not really afford it*
- *someone would be upset by their decision (maybe they should have consulted a partner beforehand)*
- *they felt overly pressured into saying 'yes'*

So, the transaction is cancelled. It doesn't affect the salespeople too much because they are used to it. Their job is to get the initial signature – if the idiot customer then cancels, that's not their fault! On to the next prospect!

> Do you see selling as a continual battle, a mental wrestling match that you have to win by forcing your opponent to sign on the dotted line? Do you have a high rate of initial success, only to be disappointed as 'buyer's remorse' kicks in?

Truly great salespeople spend their time finding out what it is that their customer wants, and then trying to match their product to the expectation. And here's a piece of heresy: you will not always be able to sell a potential client the right product! In such a case, a bad salesperson lies and bullies and twists the facts – he's going to get the sale any way he can. The new breed of successful salesperson will be honest, maybe even recommending another supplier.

> " *I'd always wanted a Mercedes and, once my business started to be successful, I went to the showroom to enquire about the cheapest in the range. The salesman was incredible – he told me that, for the money, I'd be better off with their rival's car. I always remembered that, and when I had the money after a couple more years, I went back to the garage and bought a top of the range model.* "
>
> **– Ken Levertov, publisher**

There's certainly nothing to be said for pressuring customers into the close. Success is rooted in knowing how your customers tick and understanding their needs.

Get it right with your customers

1. Forget the old image of the "talk 'em to death" salesperson. Good salespeople do more listening than talking.
2. Don't see selling in terms of confrontation. Work with, not against, your customer!
3. Be honest at all times with your customers – never give in to temptation to bend the truth for the purpose of a short-term sale.
4. If you don't feel that you can really supply what they want, give them some help in finding it elsewhere. Your honesty and openness will make them remember you in the future.

Chapter 3 — Changing Your Approach

What's in this chapter for you

Learning to like and be liked
Asking the right questions
Diary of a bad sell 2
Work on your attitude
Gathering intelligence
Before you meet the buyer

> *I always imagined that great sales people were born with the gift of the gab. I came out of university with an engineering degree, and the only job I could find at the time was in sales support. I was naturally shy, but became more confident with people as I realised they wanted to listen to my technical expertise. I'm now in charge of world-wide sales, which I still sometimes find incredible! All I do is be straight with people, honest and trustworthy, and try to get on with them. It works!*
> **– Eric Cole, sales director**

The truth is that there is no such thing as a great or a poor salesperson: there are simply great people persons and those that aren't. Eric's example above proves this perfectly.

> *There is a massive distinction between a salesperson and a people person. Whenever I am addressing our reps and agents, I make the point that some eighty per cent of all sales come from people that the potential consumer likes or is a friend of. Now that may sound soft, or even slightly hippie, but it all fits in with concepts of business partnerships.*
> **– Eric Cole**

If you are floundering in your sales career, not closing enough deals, then your problem is that you are not opening enough sales properly and you are not asking enough of the right questions.

People buy people! To become a great salesperson you therefore have to become a great people person. Nine times out of ten, when you tell salespeople this, it draws a blank, quizzical stare. It confuses a lot of them because it goes against the doctrine they have been used to, namely talking and closing.

True Story

Whilst I was writing this book the phone rang.

"Mr Webster?"

"Yes"

"My name is . . ."

He then read his spiel from a script for two minutes solidly, without stopping even for breath, desperately trying to persuade me to buy ad space in what I knew was an unsuitable medium.

"Do you think this might be of interest to you?" he said, eventually.

It was patently obvious he did not have a clue what business I was in, and therefore did not know what my requirements might be.

"If I could show you a way of selling your product to me, and generally enhancing your success rate, would you be interested in finding out how?" I responded.

" . . . errr, yes," he stammered, totally thrown.

I asked him quite a few more questions and we had a really good conversation. It turned out that he wasn't very good at what he was doing; because he was so nervous, he was totally reliant on his script. Consequently, there was no spontaneity at all in anything he was saying – he was just a detached voice on the end of the phone.

He then pre-ordered a copy of this book. I didn't fill his advertising space, but mainly because it was not suitable. I am sure that I will hear more from him.

Changing your attitude

It isn't the 'talking and closing' method that works at all. It is, indeed, the opposite that works: opening and asking questions, and showing yourself to be a real person, not a pre-scripted automaton. It is how you start and then where you go from there that can make you a great salesperson.

CHANGING YOUR APPROACH

> If, right at this moment in time, every object around you suddenly started to change colour and shape then you would have to suspend your beliefs about the laws of physics. It's not physics that we're interested in now, but you need to start thinking about, and believing in, a totally new way of looking at selling and customers. Open your mind!

Having an open mind will help you to take in the information in this book as if it were your first ever sales lesson. It will allow you to appreciate and remember that there are three phases to any sales meeting; somewhat akin to every interaction that has ever happened and ever will happen in your life. There is the before, the during and the after.

Let's start with one of the areas most often overlooked by the majority of salespeople: the before.

> *" When I'm training sales people I use the following military analogy: "If you were the commander of a group of forces due to attack someone's territory, the first thing you might do is send the scouts into the terrain to suss out the territory. You would also use your intelligence services to provide you with as much extra information as possible." They look at me initially like I'm some kind of crazed paramilitary, but in the end they learn to value the importance of thinking and planning before they go into sales meetings. "*
> **– Jeff Jenkins, sales trainer**

The motto of the British Army Intelligence Corps is *Manui Dat Cognitio Vires*, which translates as 'knowledge gives strength to the arm'. More colloquially, we all accept that 'it's brains, not brawn' that very often wins the day.

Make customer notes personal

> *" It just astounds me how many sales people don't bother to prepare properly for their appointments – it's so simple to do a little research on the company, find out some basic*

twenty-one

background information, if only to save time when you're in there and make yourself look professional. But, incredibly, very few people do it, or consider it important. "

— **Jeff Jenkins**

Proper preparation is important in any sales presentation. This may sound blindingly obvious, but amazingly few sales people seem to find the time to discover the basics about the company environment that they are going into.

> How much more confident might you feel going into a sales presentation if you knew exactly what sort of person or people you were going to be meeting? If you were visiting a company, how would you feel about some inside information on the company's short-, mid- and long-term strategic and financial planning, and the possible implications for your product or services?

" *I always enjoyed going to see Widgets Inc. and got on very well with their office services guy, Rupert. However, last time I visited, I noticed somebody opening a small box with the word MODEM printed all over it. I started my sales presentation really confidently – my fax machines had a great spec and were at unbeatable prices. But Rupert stopped me in full flow – his company had a new policy of replacing just about all their faxes with fax–modem add-ons to their PCs. Oh for a little advance information!* "

— **Karen Sharpe, office equipment representative**

You don't have to be a super sleuth or a spy to gain advance information. What Karen should have done is to have talked to her customer in advance on the phone and asked what the company policy was. If her contact wasn't available, then the receptionist or secretary would probably have been able to help her.

CHANGING YOUR APPROACH

> **"** *By not being prepared, and frankly being a bit complacent about my relationship with the customer, I really mucked things up. I wasted his time and my own, and at the same time made myself look very stupid.* **"**
> – **Karen Sharpe**

You simply have to ask questions in advance: suss things out a little. If you were going on a blind date, wouldn't you try to find out as much as you possibly could about the person beforehand? If you were about to go on holiday to somewhere new, surely you would check it out in advance. If you were about to play in the final of a competition you would certainly sound out the opposition.

It is just the same in sales.

There are two areas that you need to suss out before any meeting.

- ❑ *Firstly, you need to know as much about* **the company**, *and the industry, as possible:*
  —what are its plans and policy in relation to your product or service?
  —what are its competitors doing?
  —might there be budgetary restraints?
- ❑ *The second area is* **the individual** *you will be seeing.* Start with the most fundamental question of all: Does this person have the authority to buy your product or service?

Let's deal first with the company itself. Most businesses by law have to file their end-of-year accounts with Companies House or the local equivalent. There is some very useful information available here, ranging from the directors and their shareholding within the company to the size of its turnover over the past three years. Some libraries also hold information on companies which have had court judgements against them and, if not, then there are agencies which do have such details. (This kind of information could be useful if you have not dealt with a company before and you don't have a proper credit control department at your disposal.)

twenty-three

Many companies produce literature which will tell you nearly everything you need to know about them, such as when they started, where they are going, and who does what. Look on the internet – a lot of larger companies have web sites that can tell you an immense amount about their products or services they provide and the personnel involved.

> *" Obviously I can't do it for every customer, but when I'm trying to get into new businesses, I now phone them up and ask for as much of their free information as possible. It really helps me to get an inside view of their business and to be prepared for the first meeting. "*
> **– Karen Sharpe**

When ringing up to make your appointment, it is also a good opportunity to glean a few more facts. Receptionists and secretaries are always a mine of information and are normally glad to impart some of it, as long as they feel that they are not being disloyal or giving away anything confidential.

Making an ally out of the secretary can be a very wise move. If you do it well you will have someone rooting for your cause from the outset. A lot of bosses have good relationships with their secretaries and PAs, and are likely to be influenced if they hear from them that you seem like a reliable, pleasant and honest person.

All you have to do is ask the right kind questions, questions pertaining to your task in hand. Examples might be:

- How many employees do they have who use your kind of products or services?
- What is their company policy in relation to your business?
- What is the management hierarchy?
- Who are their current suppliers?

Make the effort to find out as much information as you can – it will help you enormously.

CHANGING YOUR APPROACH

Also ask about the people you are going to see:

- Do they like quick appointments or long ones?
- Have they been in that job for a long time or are they rising meteorically up the corporate ladder?
- Do they make the decisions or do they need to ask someone else? (This is very important because you may not even have the appointment with the right person.)
- Can you expect to be given an order then or there, or is there a requisition procedure to be followed?

> *When the moment arrives to turn up for the appointment, I aim to have a reasonable understanding of the company, its turnover, the size of its potential market, who its competitors are and what they are investing in. If I also have some basic information about the individual whom I'll be seeing, then that really helps too. Advance information helps give me just that little bit more confidence, and that slight edge.*
> **– Karen Sharpe**

And remember, treat everyone you meet in a friendly and courteous manner – you never know when this might come in useful!

> *One of my biggest long-standing customers had a large open-plan buying office, and from day one I made sure that I got to know everyone's name, regardless of whether they were simply support staff with no buying power. What has gradually happened is that many of the younger people are now buyers, and my relationship has been good with them from the start. You'd be amazed, but one now senior buyer has even told me that, when she was just an administrator, many of the reps treated her like a dogsbody! She's getting her own back now!*
> **– Marvin Peters, sales agent**

All you have to do is a little homework to suss it all out beforehand, and be aware that you are dealing with real people – treat them as such. This will give you both a tremendous knowledge advantage and also should serve to increase your own confidence. It's a great way to go into your meeting.

twenty-five

The power of proper preparation will quickly prove itself to you. If you don't already put 100 per cent effort into preparing for meetings, start NOW.

1. Plan each and every sales call you have to make. Know precisely why you are there, who you are seeing and what you aim to achieve.
2. Look around you in companies. Make friends, ask questions and start to get a feel for the kind of business you are trying to sell to.
3. Secretaries and receptionists can prove valuable allies. Try to develop your relationships with them; it could pay dividends in the future.
4. When visiting new clients, find out as much as you can about them beforehand. This will impress them, save you valuable selling time and give you a big knowledge advantage.

LEARNING SUSS — Chapter 4

What's in this chapter for you

- **First impressions count**
- **Starting to SUSS**
- **Looking and feeling the part**
- **State of mind**
- **Golden handshakes**
- **Understudying**
- **Body language**
- **Mind methods**

> *❝ You don't get a second chance to make a good first impression. ❞*
> **– Marvin Peters**

That's the adage. It's not always true, but it is hard to reverse an initial bad impression.

Modern human beings have inherited from our prehistoric ancestors the need to make a quick and accurate judgement on whether another is a friend or foe. This genetic 'fight or flight' response is designed to protect our well-being.

Perhaps not as necessary as it was thousands of years ago in terms of life or death, it does still govern the opening of the majority of first meetings. Whether you are attempting to fit into a group of potential new friends, meeting a potential new partner in a relationship or in your business dealings, you are up against people who have an in-built need to make a quick assessment of you!

> *❝ My major supplier took on a new representative a couple of years back, and he made an appointment to see me. Well, maybe I'm old fashioned, but I took an instant dislike to him. He wore a flashy suit, loud tie and tried greeting me like a long-lost friend. To make matters worse, he had no idea about my core business. I'm afraid I changed suppliers shortly after. ❞*
> **– George Horton, farmer**

twenty-seven

Would you buy a new kitchen from a greasy-haired salesman wearing a stained suit and sandals?

Dressing the part, looking the part and acting the part are as important as being the part – and, as we will come on to, listening the part – in making that first impression a good one. To do this you have to be in the correct state of mind.

To help you remember the key four-step process of approaching the meeting itself, we are going to use the acronym SUSS as a reminder.

The first S of SUSS

This stands for your state – your *State of body* and your *State of mind*.

There is a saying that goes 'everyone loves a winner', and it is true of the majority of people. The first indication of whether you are a winner or a loser is your external appearance, how you dress and how you carry yourself, the aura that you give off.

George's feed rep above made the fundamental mistake of turning up in what George assumed to be clothing inappropriate to a farm. Now we are not suggesting that he should have dressed as if he had just cleaned out the pigs, but he could have chosen smart comfortable clothes that fitted the environment in which he was working.

How you dress and the other elements of your physical appearance should be a matter of common sense. Pay attention to it, for you will never climb the ladder of success dressed in the clothes of failure.

Here's a brief clothing checklist that will help ensure you get the happy balance:

- Make sure your clothes fit – just because you could fit into your favourite suit in 1988, it doesn't necessarily mean it will fit you today!
- Check your hair and other elements of your appearance such as your fingernails; it makes a difference.
- Avoid loud flashy items of clothing, and take off over-the-top jewellery. Many people regard loudness as unsavoury or even threatening.
- Try to dress to match the customer you are visiting. So, if you are going to a hi-tech head office account, your sharpest clothes are appropriate. If you are visiting a small local company who you know have a casual dress code, wear smart but casual clothing.
- Make sure that your clothes are clean and odour free. If you are a smoker, try not to light up in the confined space of your car as you will smell of tobacco, and that can put a huge number of people off.

What your clothing and grooming should be doing is to make your potential client think at first sight that you are similar to them.

Your internal *State* – how you come across as a person, your attitude or state of mind – is the next important factor. A false state of mind won't do. It is like a veneer that will wear thin and flake off very quickly.

> The *State* of mind that will serve both you and your potential customer extremely well is one of being about to meet someone who may well become a life-long friend; someone who you would wish to do things for, and whom you would hope would also do things for you.

This *State* of mind will assist you enormously but it may well have the added bonus that you do indeed become friends. What a great way to do business in the future! Go to lunch with a friend, enjoy the food and the company, and tidy up a little paperwork at the end of the meal by taking a large order!

> ❝ *I've been on the road now for twenty-five years, and seen sales managers and directors come and go. I've been offered management jobs myself, but I've never been tempted,*

mainly because I'd miss most of my customers too much. I count them as friends, I socialise with them, but always get the business done. I know some people in the head office think I may be past it, but my figures are always excellent and most of my customers could not envisage doing business with my company unless it was through me. It might seem like an old-fashioned way to do business, but it works and I still enjoy it! **"**
– George McQuaid, publisher's representative

What character attributes or mental *State* makes a great first impression on you and how would you display those attributes, even when you have had a miserable day?

Let's be honest, if you've got trouble at home, hassle with the children, or are simply not feeling 100 per cent, then it can be difficult to motivate yourself to be the efficient, pleasant professional you know you should be.

Here's how one sales professional gets herself into the right frame of mind:

" *I used to find it difficult to pump myself up for some meetings – especially if it was the end of the week, when I was tired and I knew the traffic on the way home was going to be a nightmare! But I've now tried to adopt a state of mind where I am about to meet the brother or sister of someone I used to have a very good friendship with: I'm really looking forward to the meeting; I'm confident, without being cocky; I'm eager to ask questions; and I'm a great listener. People like me, and I fully expect this person to like me. Not only am I a nice person but I also deliver value and I deliver solutions as opposed to a product or service. Also, I have a genuinely great smile! I know it is going to be an interesting and fruitful experience.* **"**
– Rachel James, sales consultant

So, how can you create this state of mind or attitude when you are having a hellish day and would really rather be at home nursing a large gin and tonic?

> A good technique to get yourself into the right State of mind is as follows:
>
> - ❏ *Take five minutes to yourself before each sales call to relax.*
> - ❏ *Breathe deeply, and start thinking about something you do well, either professionally or in your private life. It doesn't matter what it is and it needn't be a difficult task. Something simple will do.*
> - ❏ *As you think about whatever it is that you do well, think about a time when you felt very confident about something you were about to do. Again, it could be leisure or work related.*
> - ❏ *Now, remember how you felt when you achieved success. It could be a prize at school, a job offer after a superb interview performance or a sporting achievement. Try to recapture your feelings of glory.*
> - ❏ *Assume the body posture of someone who is supremely confident. How do they stand or sit? Maybe you could pretend that you are your favourite confident movie star.*
> - ❏ *Breathe deeply and imagine yourself walking out of your next call with the order in your hand.*

Repeat the above process with the other attributes that may be useful to you. For instance, you could remember a time when you were very compassionate and did something very kind for someone else. Build up the feelings, sights and sounds that were associated with it, praise yourself for being a warm-hearted person and step into your State.

Remember a time when you were totally intrigued by someone and were totally enraptured by what they had to say. Build up the intensity of the experience and step into your State.

> Do this with all of the attributes that you think will help you. Practise this technique in quiet moments as much as you can and next time you are about to enter a meeting just step into your imaginary State. Allow it to engulf you.

thirty-one

If you make a commitment to yourself to learn and practise this particular technique then you will learn how to change your state of mind at a moment's notice, particularly when you most need to.

Remember to do it with your smile too. A genuine smile is the most important representation of both your internal and external states.

Handshakes

The first physical contact you will have with the person you are meeting will be a handshake, unless you are *very* good friends or an Eskimo. This is terribly important process when aiming to make a good first impression.

If you have developed a standard handshake, abandon it. It is vitally important to return, match and complement the handshake of the other person.

There are three main types of handshake: the limp fish, the neutral and the vice.

If you squash their limp fish with your vice they will immediately feel overpowered and very different from you. If you place your limp fish into their vice, the same applies, but in reverse, and they will once again feel as though you are very different from them.

> " *I am a small woman, and I get so cross when great big men get all macho with me by virtually squashing my hand when we meet. What are they trying to prove? Why can't they can shake my hand firmly without reshaping my wedding ring?* "
> – **Sue Hopper, senior buyer**

Start with the neutral handshake and soften or harden as necessary. It is the first chance you will get to persuade the subconscious mind of the other person to make a quick assumption that you are similar to each other.

LEARNING SUSS

The Understudy

The next letter in the acronym SUSS is U and this stands for *Understudy*.

This is the key word to helping you to do the next most important thing within the sales process, and also to make new friends. It is one of the keys to becoming a great people person; creating rapport with a total stranger.

> " *The best salesperson on the team is the quietest and most mild mannered. George has an effortless charm with people, and just comes across as a really nice guy. He's not soft or anything, and fills his order book better than anyone else, but what is interesting is that he does it by empathising fully with the customer.* "
> **– Anne Kelly, sales manager**

George's talent probably hinges on one simple and indisputable fact – **people who are like each other tend to like each other**. You can twist it any which way you like and it still has the same impact. Try it backwards: people who like each other tend to be like each other.

> Have you ever noticed how two people who have a complete rapport with each other seem to be almost copying or *Understudying* each other? They are perhaps sitting at a table in a restaurant, facing each other, in an identical position, and probably quite close to each other. They are almost certainly talking at the same pace and even breathing at the same rate.

Conversely, we've all seen couples who do not seem to have a rapport with each other.

thirty-three

Have you noticed how differently two people can behave when they are together? Often you'll see one of them has his or her elbows on the table and is leaning forwards. The other person is sitting back in their chair, legs crossed, arms folded with one hand covering their jaw. That person is giving slow, deliberate answers whilst the other person is jabbering away excitedly, words pouring out ten to the dozen, arms waving about rapidly. Do you think that they are in rapport with each other?

The key, therefore, to creating a rapport with a person, stranger or otherwise, is to *Understudy* them – like an actor or actress must understudy someone, ready to step into his or her role at a moment's notice – and be like the other person.

Communicating

The starting point here is to understand that everyone has a different method of communicating with themselves and with others; a different *mind method*. The second point is to understand that communication itself is not just about the words that people use. Indeed, in external communication, words are the least important of all.

If your partner came up to you, wrapped his or her arms around you, gently stroked your back, looked deeply and lovingly into your eyes and said "I really hate you . . .", what message might you be getting? How important would his or her actual words be?

The fact is that only seven per cent of our communication is through the words that we use. A much larger percentage, thirty-eight to be precise, is through the intonation and voice inflection that we use, and by far the most important part of our communication is through our body language.

Body language is all about facial expression, body posture, breathing patterns, and arm and hand movements.

LEARNING SUSS

> *" I pride myself on being good at understanding and reading the body language of all of the reps I see in here. Some sit timidly arms folded and that is a sign to me of nervousness and fear. If I need to I can bully the right deal out of someone like that. If someone else quotes me a price but doesn't make eye contact, then I know that they are not telling me everything and that they can give me a better deal. It's a skill which can be learnt on training courses but I've just picked it up from watching and studying people. It gives me a huge advantage. "*
> – **Joan Stimac, senior buyer**

If you were late home one night and you see your partner waiting for you at the door, standing tall, arms folded, scowling, eyes glowering – you can almost see steam coming out of the ears – then let me ask you a question: do you need any verbal communication to get the gist of what is going through their mind? And did you remember to wear your body armour!?

What about that little eye roll that says 'what a fool he is making of himself'. One hundred per cent communication with one gesture!

Now that you understand the importance of body posture and body movement, let's go back to those *mind methods*.

Most of us interpret and process all communication through our three major senses of sight, sound and feel. Nearly every one of you has chosen to adopt one of these three senses as your predominant method or tool for communicating and interpreting your world. You are almost certainly either a *visual person*, an *auditory person* or a *kinaesthetic person*.

It is important, as you will see later, to recognise which one of these types of people you are. Look at the following series of questions to find out.

> Do you get an 'insight' into things? Do you tend to have a 'viewpoint' on certain matters? Do you like to get the 'picture'? Do you tend to talk quite quickly and use a lot of gesticulations? Do you say 'I see what you mean?'

If this seems to be you then you are predominantly a *visual* person.

> Do you like to talk things through? Is it important for you to get 'attuned' to things? Do you often say 'I hear what you are saying'? Do things 'ring a bell'? Are you 'all ears' when with others? Do you tend to listen closely to other people's words to hear exactly what they are saying? Do you speak at a fairly moderate pace and not use a lot of fast body language?

If this seems to be you then you are predominantly an *auditory* person.

Do neither of the above seem to fit you?

> Do you like to get hold of the situation and gain control of it? Do you like to weigh things up before you get a handle on it? As you are doing this, do you usually speak quite slowly and deliberately, weighing all options up before giving an opinion?

If this fits you best, then you are a *kinaesthetic* person, someone who likes to get a feel for things.

Many people are a hybrid of all three of these, but are nearly always predominantly one type or other on given occasions.

> Whether you are trying to sell something, trying to make a new friend or even trying to find a potential partner, the critically important thing to realise is this: if you are a *visual* person, who likes to get from A to B quickly, you will not like the speed at which *kinaesthetic* people communicate and will not get a feel for them (or their products). You will find it very difficult to understand what they are getting at, because they will communicate in very different ways to yourself.

Similarly, the *auditory* person doesn't like *kinaesthetic* people, who keep going on about 'feeling' things; and *visual* people, who insist on 'seeing' things, will always be a bit of a mystery. He will think these other people are on a different planet and will be wanting to tune into a few bits of language that he can interpret.

The poor *kinaesthetic* will have to try desperately to get to grips with *visual* people, who talk at hyper-speed, wave their arms around, spout benefits and seem to use a foreign language all the time while incessantly asking 'do you get the picture?'.

So, hopefully you will be able to identify what kind of person you are, and to recognise your behavioural patterns.

> Using the above definitions, ask someone close to you what kind of person they think you are. Now, look at your close friends or loved ones. Are they the same or similar to you? The chances are, they will be, or you will both modify your behaviour to match each other when together.

" Whenever I meet a potential client, I study them. I make mental notes about how they talk, both in terms of their intonation and the kind of language they use, then I try to adopt a similar way of communicating. I find that the rapport is built much more quickly, and conversation and information flows much more easily. I'm not claiming that this gives me a 100 per

cent success rate, but generally my sales are highest in the team. **"**
– Gary Hart, pensions advisor

To be liked by someone, you have to be like them. If you as a person are the complete opposite of your potential customer, then you are going to find it incredibly difficult to get anywhere with him or her.

To create a rapport with a potential customer you have to study them and then understudy them.

In NLP, the study of communication, this is known as matching and mirroring. When you enter another person's environment you need to fit into that environment as quickly as possible, otherwise you will stand out like an old grandfather clock in a modern state-of-the-art office suite (you can probably tell from that metaphor that I am a visual person!).

> **ACT!** To gain the trust of your potential clients and build a rapport, you need to communicate like them. Pick up their pace as if you were both going on a long journey together. They lead and you follow alongside.

Tips for matching and mirroring

- *Adopt the body posture of the other person, every last bit of it. Look at how they are standing or sitting, and mirror it. As they move and change theirs then so too should you change yours to match it.*
- *Match their facial expressions and any body movement. If they lean forward then you lean forward and if they start tapping the desk then pick up their rhythmic speed and tap your other hand or your knee at the same tempo and rhythm.*
- *Pick up the tempo of how they are speaking. If they are speaking slowly and deliberately, then do the same. If they use metaphors, or strongly descriptive language, then try to do so yourself.*
- *If they are casual in their language, using slang or colloquialisms, do the same (but avoid the temptation to impersonate their accent – remember Dick van Dyke in Mary Poppins!).*

LEARNING SUSS

> **ACT!** If you overdo matching and mirroring, it could seem like mimicking and will come across as manipulative. But just watch any couple who are have a full rapport with one another, like the two in the restaurant we discussed earlier. As one of them shifts position, so too the other will follow. This rapport is at the subconscious level and is the most natural of all. It is this natural ease that you should be aiming for.

If you repeat the same process for the speed and pitch at which you talk, the intonation you use and the words that you use, your potential client's subconscious will say to itself: "This person is just like me". Remember that most people tend to like others who are like them.

> **ACT!** Experiment with changing a part of your communication and and see if people follow you. If they do then you know you have established a rapport. This can also be a lot of fun!

When you eventually master the art of picking up and matching someone's pace and mind method and being just like them, you can then even lead them to pick up your pace. When you have a complete rapport you can then lead them elsewhere. You have gained their trust. Try this with someone you know. Pace them, match them and then lead them.

> **TIPS**
>
> ### The foundations of SUSSing other people
>
> 1. Try to blend in with whatever environment you find yourself in. The first thing to start with is your clothing. Don't be tempted to wear an Armani suite if your customer will be wearing oil-stained overalls.
> 2. Make sure you feel comfortable in your clothes – look good and you'll probably feel good. Vary your wardrobe from smart-formal to smart-casual but avoid the downright scruffy!

TIPS

3. Accept that you are not always going to feel bright and breezy, and ready to sell a million. Learn how to change your moods – think of previous successes, situations where you have been on top form, and recapture the feelings you experienced then.
4. Learn to smile! It's the first thing people will notice and a great smile will get you off to a flying start.
5. Don't use your handshake as an offensive weapon. Even if you are built like the side of a house, moderate your handshake to match that of the person you are meeting. Similarly, if two wet fish are attached to your wrists, then work on making them strong wet fish – don't get crushed!
6. Analyse other people's behaviour and learn to match and mirror it. Look at their posture, and sit or stand to complement them.
7. Learn to recognise what kind of person others are. Are they *visual*, *auditory* or *kinaesthetic*? What kind of person are you? Learn to mirror and match.
8. Remember – people like others who are like them.

Seek And Ye Shall Find

— Chapter 5

What's in this chapter for you

Seeking the right information
What people want when they buy
Selling benefits, not boxes
The right way to ask questions
Giving Satisfaction
A little about product knowledge

The second S in SUSS

The third letter in the acronym SUSS is S and it stands for *Seek*.

The ability to *seek* information and then to deliver solutions is the key to successful selling. The ability to understand and practise this is what sets great salespeople apart.

In that ancient book of wisdom, the Bible, it is written 'Seek and ye shall find'. However, most sales literature which has been written over the years is built around the 'convince' ethic; it is based on the theory that you overcome objections and convince the customer that yours is the right product. The scripture according to this theory could be rewritten as 'bully and ye might sell'.

> Throw away all of your preconceived ideas about selling being a job of convincing. Adopt the frame of mind or attitude that you are a *seeker* and not a convincer. By doing so, you will write more orders than ever before and the selling process will become a much more gratifying and rewarding process for both you and for your client.

So what is it that you should be seeking?

Nobody, but nobody, buys a car just because they want a car. Nobody buys a conservatory because they want a conservatory. Nobody buys an investment or life policy because they want such a policy. Nobody buys advertising space because they covet advertising space. What they do buy is what it does for them,

forty-one

what value it creates for them in their life or for their business — what solution it offers.

ACT! — You should always be seeking for the dominant reason or motive that makes someone desire your product or service.

> " *Whatever your product may be, people buy the value that that product or service offers, not the means value but the end-value. The car itself is the means value. What it does for you is the end-value. It is the end-value that really counts and that's what I keep permanently in my mind.* "
> **– Ron Crawford, car dealership owner**

Think back to the last time you purchased a car. Something made you purchase that particular vehicle. It may have been the speed it does or alternatively its fuel consumption figures. It may have been that you felt particularly safe in this car or maybe a luxury interior made you think that here was an environment that you could spend time in. It may have been that you could imagine certain people being jealous of your car. It may simply have been that it was the right price. Whatever it was, something was important to you. There was a deeper reason, some end-value, that motivated you to buy that particular car.

> " *I remember when I first owned a car, I was just delighted to have an object to get me from A to B. Now that I'm quite successful, I look for other things. Firstly, I want comfort and safety for my family. Secondly, and if I'm being honest this is a crucial consideration, I want something which reflects my success and that shows people I am a man of means. I'm afraid the A to B bit is way down my list of priorities now.* "
> **– Ron Crawford**

It is hard to get all excited about spending one tenth of your income to own a piece of paper with 'Policy Document' printed on it. It is, however, possible to get excited about retiring early, going on a round-the-world cruise, and knowing that there will always be enough money and financial security to keep you in, or enhance, the lifestyle that you are used to. For another person that same document may mean something totally different. It may create a totally different end-value.

Selling the benefits

You need to *seek* from your potential clients their prime motive for even considering making a purchase. They may not even know what that motive is themselves, in which case it is down to you to find out. To do so, you need to look at people's perceptions of the product and the kind of language used.

Let's look at people's perceptions of buying advertising space in magazines or journals. With the rather quirky attitude that many companies and individuals have towards off-the-page advertising, selling 'space' is a very difficult business to be in and usually has a very high level of staff turnover (look at all the 'publishing sales jobs' advertised in the recruitment section of any newspaper). Or is it? Maybe it's a simple case of terminology.

Buying 'space' is a strange term: there is loads of space out there – just look up towards the sky at night time. Surely you'd agree that it would sound more worth while to say:

- *Buying increased company profile*
- *Buying in business*
- *Buying in customers*
- *Buying the opportunity to increase income*
- *Buying in security for yourself*

> **Think in terms of what the product offers to potential buyers. You will then be starting to sell its benefits, not just the product itself.**

ACT!

So, before you even start plugging your product, you need to find out what is going to motivate your potential customers to buy. Information, therefore, has to be of critical importance. In order to gain information you have seek it; you have to ask questions.

forty-three

SUPER SELLING WITH NLP

> " *Many of my salespeople used to just talk. I noticed that the very best would ask questions and then* **shut up** *and* **listen** *to the answers. By asking the right questions and listening carefully to the answers you will gain all of the information you need to enable you progress to the final stage and get the business. This is the now at the heart of our sales training.* "
>
> **– Ron Crawford**

So, as well as asking questions, you have to listen to the answers.

Just suppose for a moment that you sell conservatories for a living. You are in the home of the prospective clients and you have built a good rapport with them. You also know that they are very visual people. What questions might you ask?

You don't have to be a genius to remember all of these, because there are basically only two. The first of these is "What is important to you?".

So the question goes *"What is important to you about having your own conservatory?"*

Let us say that the first answer is *"I see it as somewhere nice to go on an evening"*.

Okay. So now you know that evenings in the conservatory are important to them. Do not think that this is their end-value: it's only a half-way house.

"And what does that mean to you?" is the next question to ask.

"Well, it means that I can get away from work and relax. I could go in there, watch the world go by and gaze up at the stars at night."

Now we are getting there. Notice, too, how all of a sudden he has gone all kinaesthetic. Let's ask the question again and add two important words from the hypnotherapist's dictionary – as you.

"As you see yourself sitting there, watching the stars, what does that make you feel?"

You may well get an answer such as *"Well, I just see myself totally at one with the world. It's when I do my most creative thinking too."*

SEEK AND YE SHALL FIND

Bingo. This man doesn't want a conservatory. He wants to sit behind some glass, watch the stars, get in touch with himself and do some creative thinking.

> You may have to ask many questions to build up the full picture or the gut feel for your client. To do this, simply ask similar follow-up questions:
>
> ❑ *"What else is important to you about having a .....?"* then
> ❑ *"What does that mean to you?"*

⟶ **ACT!**

People love to talk, and be listened to. It's one of the fundamental laws of psychology. Don't be afraid to ask lots of questions. Furthermore, they are now doing your job for you. They are telling you their deep-seated reasons for wanting your product. They are literally selling it to themselves.

You can then round it all up: *"Of all the things you just mentioned, what is most important of all?"*

The answer to this question should tell you what their highest end-value of all is and how that will relate to your product. It is the most important piece of information you need. You are now ready to move on to the final stage.

The final S

The last letter in the acronym SUSS is another S.

"But where is the 'C'", you might ask if you are already a sales person; "it all makes perfect sense so far, but what about the *close*; you have to close the deal don't you?"

In my opinion the word should be eliminated from all sales training forever. It is a really negative word. Who the heck likes to be *closed*, locked in, strapped up . . . how would you feel about having just been 'closed' into a deal? It's no wonder that many people get buyer's remorse a short while after being closed.

> *Of course you have to take an order: that's the job of everybody in sales. 'Taking the order', however, is a much more pleasant set of circumstances than 'going for the close' or 'being closed'. The traditional method of 'closing' suggests a conflict: pitting your wits against the customers'. It is far less threatening to think in terms of taking an order to open up new possibilities. Surely that is what you are doing if you believe in your product or service; you are opening up a whole new world of possibilities for your customer.*
> – **Ron Crawford**

Ron is 100 per cent right. I believe that this attitude or thought process will revolutionise your approach and really increase your order-taking rate.

Before you take the order there is one last thing you must do. You have to *Satisfy* the customers' criteria for purchasing your product or service, and you also have to *Satisfy* the 'ecology', or the consequences, of their decision.

If your potential customer is obviously champing at the bit to order your product, because he or she likes you so much and has answered so many of the right questions that they have sold it to themselves, then simply ask for the order. At this stage you may well have satisfied the customer's criteria already.

ACT! — If the sale is all but agreed, ask a very simple question: "Would you like to get the paperwork out of the way now, or in a moment or two?"

JARGON buster — The question "Would you like to get the paperwork out of the way now, or in a moment or two?" is called a **time bind**. This is a technique learnt and adapted from the greatest neural linguist of our time, Milton H. Erickson. It is so clever because it offers a choice, but the choice has the same end result. The choice is whether to order it now or in a moment or two. If the customer doesn't say "Yes" now, he or she has just agreed to say "Yes" in a moment or two.

SEEK AND YE SHALL FIND

With a "Yes" response to your time bind, you just have a few more criteria to satisfy before the customer makes the decision.

Many people are afraid of making decisions. Indeed most human beings hate having to make their minds up. Studies have shown that we suffer temporary insanity prior to making decisions. The reason for this is that most people have not considered the consequences of the decision: whether or not they can afford it; whether some other person might be unhappy about the decision. There are of course a whole host of consequences that may be on the mind of your customer. The consequences of the reliability of your product or the effectiveness of your service, plus its shape, size, suitability, weight, packaging, colour, quality, reliability and longevity, could all influence the decision.

> If you feel totally happy with the consequences of a decision that you have to make then surely you would make that decision right now. But, what would you think about if you were making a decision to make a major purchase?

If customers do not want to order straight away, you have not satisfied their qualms about the consequences of the decision.

The next question to ask always starts with the same five words: *what would have to happen . . .?*

Link these five words to their highest end-value – which you should have established earlier – and use words suitable to their 'mind method' and phrase a question something like this: *"What would have to happen for you take the first step towards being in your conservatory, watching the world go by, being at one with things and being very creative?"*

> When you ask hesitant customers what must happen for them to be able to make their decision, listen very carefully to their answer, for it will be full of clues.

forty-seven

As well as having a mind method, everyone also has a set of 'motivation methods' or 'mind methodologies'. These range from whether people need to do something for themselves or for the approval of others to whether they need their product to be the same as other people's or different.

The methodology I will now briefly explain is the most powerful one of them all, and understanding and using this will give you a great edge.

Everything you ever do and every decision that you ever make is aimed at an outcome which either gives you pleasure or avoids you suffering pain. There are virtually no exceptions to this rule. In terms of 'mind methodology', most people choose to make decisions based upon moving towards something pleasurable or moving away from something painful.

When you ask a question of someone they will, by and large, answer it in one of two ways. They will tell you what they do want or what they don't want.

"I want to do XYZ because it will give me ABC." This person moves towards pleasure.

"I don't want to do XYZ because otherwise I won't get ABC." This person moves away from pain.

> Do you recognise the pleasure gain/pain avoidance distinction in what people say? For instance, think of the people who will get in the car and drive half a mile because they enjoy driving whilst others will think of the drive in terms of 'they hate walking'.

These two methods of thinking are diametrically opposed to one another. It is important to listen to the wording of people's answers and phrase your next question using their mind methodology.

Answer one might be "I would have to be sure that I wasn't going to be left in financial trouble." This is a moving away strategy. Your next question would therefore be "If I could show how to

SEEK AND YE SHALL FIND

purchase this product in a way that would not leave you in any financial trouble, would you then be ready to order it?"

The other answer might be *"I want to make sure that I can afford it."* This is a moving towards strategy. You would then phrase your question like this: *"If I can show you how you can afford it would you then be ready to order it?"*

Within both of these questions **if** and **then** are the key words. They do need to be matched to either the moving towards or moving away strategy of your client to be most effective when handling so-called objections. Use these two words to overcome and circumnavigate any uncertainty your potential customer may have with regard to the consequence of their decision.

If you elegantly and sincerely lead your customer to a situation whereby they are totally happy and comfortable with all of the consequences of having purchased your product or service you will then be able to take the order. The important distinction here is that you have not had to leap over a series of fences and ditches on an obstacle course in order to close a sale. All that you have done is opened up a clear route together.

Product knowledge

It's now time for just a small caveat. You may have all the charm in the world, be able to mirror and match the actions of anyone you meet and make friends quickly and easily with total strangers. However, all of this will be totally useless unless you fully understand what it is you are selling.

This can only be achieved with hard work.

> " *I sell personal pensions and recently there has been a lot of adverse publicity about people being sold unsuitable products. When I talk to a new client, it is important that I establish what end-value they are after. Do they want a nice lump sum; are they looking for the flexibility to retire early; or are they looking for a comfort level at the age of 65? Whatever it is, I need to know my range of products well enough to find something suitable for their requirements – good product knowledge is vital.* "
> **– Gary Hart**

ACT! — Commit to gaining a full understanding of the products you are trying to sell. If people ask you a question that you can't answer, don't be tempted to bluff your way out, as you could end up selling something totally inappropriate. Find out the answers, and get back to them.

If your main source of product knowledge is through sales meetings and you don't find these useful, then speak to your bosses and make suggestions as to how they can be improved and turned into learning processes.

Future benefits

We have learnt so far the importance of seeing your customers as real people, not merely as faceless employees, hiding the company cheque-book that you are desperate to get your hands on. By following the basic examples of neuro-linguistic programming, matching and mirroring behaviour and thus reaching a true rapport with everyone you meet, you can and will achieve sales success.

There are other benefits as well to be gained by this.

> *I used to have a team full of sales people spending an inordinate amount of time cold calling. Let's be honest, it's a dispiriting job, no one likes it and only outrageous bull-shitters are any good at it. We have a great product that people like, so we started asking our existing clients for referrals. It really worked – most are only too glad to recommend friends and family.*
> **– Pete Hayes, sales director**

If you've built a rapport with your customers, and have a friendly relationship with them, then ask for referrals. Can you quote them on sales literature? Who do they know in their company who might be interested in your product or service?

> *Not only do I get most of my sales leads from my existing customers, but I've also never needed to apply for other jobs. Both times I've made a move, it's because I've been*

SEEK AND YE SHALL FIND

approached by other companies as a direct result of personal recommendations from my customers. **"**
– Gary Wear, area sales manager

If you have created value and given true service before, during and after the sale, you will never need another list of potential new contacts.

How many times have you gone to a restaurant or to the movies or to seek professional advice on the recommendation of someone else? Much business is conducted in the same manner. A good quality referral, even if to someone who currently has no need for your services, may mean that you need never cold canvass again.

> Imagine you started today with that one satisfied client and turned that into two referrals and then the next day turned those two into four. How many potential referrals might you have by the end of a thirty-one day month if you could simply double the amount from the day before. I know that you probably don't know the answer but if you did know then what would it be? Take a quick guess.
> Rounding it down to a nice even figure the answer is 1,000 million referrals. Point zero one per cent of that is still a million.

From one totally satisfied client you can build an income stream for life if you continue to apply the same principals of

- ○ doing your groundwork beforehand
- ○ creating the right physical and mental **State**
- ○ **Understudying** to create rapport
- ○ becoming a seeker and not a convincer; **Seek** information as to what customers value in your product or service
- ○ and **Satisfy**ing customers' concerns about the consequences of them purchasing your product.

There is but one thing left to do. This one function or act can beneficially affect your repeat business and your quality and quantity of referrals. It is that so often ignored area of 'after-sales service'.

ACT! — Take the time to go around and visit your clients after they have received your product, or the service that you have provided is in operation, to check that they're satisfied. Offer them a little help if needed. Show them that you care and it will make an immense difference. It is also a superb opportunity to ask for that first referral.

And finally, remember that this is a framework within which to work and that all of the points in this book are guiding principles. Learning the finer points that fit into this framework will truly set you apart from the pack. Learning to adapt and be flexible in your verbal and non-verbal responses will give you that extra special edge, not just in selling, but also in all of your interactions with other people, whether it be succeeding in an interview, making new friends or finding your ideal partner.

Commit to understanding SUSS. Practise it with friends or strangers. Practise understudying, matching and mirroring others, and seek information as to what is really important to them. It is a great method of making conversation and forming new friendships.

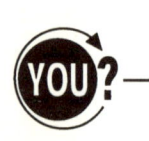

YOU? — Whether you are just leaving school or you are the chairman of a large corporation, or a single person looking for a partner, or are simply seeking to make new friends, you are constantly having to sell yourself aren't you? Flexibility is an important character trait to possess to enable you to use the principles of SUSS. Are you flexible?

I hope that you have both enjoyed and benefited from this introduction to SUSS and that it will make a significant difference to both your sales performance and to all of your dealings with your fellow men and women.

SEEK AND YE SHALL FIND

The rest of SUSS

1. Your job when selling is to *Seek* information. Why might someone want to buy your product? The only way to find out is to ask the right questions.
2. Once you've asked the right questions, shut up and listen! By doing so, and understanding what people are really saying and meaning, you will be able to find their true motivations.
3. People buy the benefits of products, not the product itself. Concentrate always on selling the benefits – what the product will do for the potential customer.
4. "Closing" the sale is the worst expression in business. Forget closing for ever – concentrate on opening instead, using the techniques of SUSS.
5. People make decisions to give themselves pleasure or to avoid pain. Listen to their responses, and find out their 'mind methods' so you can fully *Satisfy* them.
6. Know your customer, but also know your product. You can win Gold Medals in the Charm Olympics, but if you don't know your product then you will not succeed.
7. Ask for referrals from your good customers – treat them as friends who will want to help!
8. Keep in touch with customers. Database their details, and follow up on your sale to them. Find out if they're happy; can they refer you to anyone else; is there anything else in your portfolio that they may be interested in?
9. Everyone sells. SUSS techniques will help you in your professional and personal life, regardless of your job title, so use them!

If there is one over-riding message to leave you with then it is this: it is the value that you create for others in life that counts. The return will come as a pleasant by-product of that process.

Enjoy the process.

RUSSELL WEBSTER

After several years on the sales training circuit, with clients such as Rank Zerox and Allied Dunbar, Russell Webster formed Mindworld Publishing: an innovative company in the field of audio books on human nature, personal development, and training. Highly regarded as an eloquent and gifted speaker and narrator he already has several top selling audio books to his name and has three books in print with a well known publisher.

Described as a trainer who possesses 'the human touch' he has a deep understanding of human needs, human nature and motivation. His preferred area to train in is people skills, motivation, communication, sales and attitude.

Very much a right-brain, lateral and creative thinker he has also regularly been called upon, by several well-known companies, to assist in creating a new corporate identity, vision, mission and focus. He is currently working with ex-Saatchi and Saatchi man J.J.Gabay on a new book project based upon the psychology of 'influence by design'.

Russell and his fellow Directors have one core belief and that is that

Everybody is in the people business.

organisational structure, whatever it shape, is made up of people. *People* are without doubt the most important asset any organisation can have.

People originate concepts and ideas, and people create a vision. People design strategic plans and structures. People sit or stand at a production line and people make products. People market and sell products or services. People buy products or services. Any

Learning how to influence the behaviour of people will be the management art of the future.

Learning how to influence the behaviour of people's buying habits will be one of the main business arts of the future.

YOU are in the people business.

The future of your organisation will therefore depend upon two major factors:

1. Your ability to recruit, train and inform the highest quality of people. People who can work under their own initiative yet also inspire others and work within a team. People who are highly motivated and people who can motivate others. People who can contribute toward and share the vision of your organisation.

2. Your ability to influence people: your clients and potential end-users/customers. This is not just an internal marketing and sales function. It is also an external function. Old fashioned design agencies create works of art and powerful imagery - often creating the wrong association to your product or service. The future of advertising and design lies with those who understand the psychology of influencing people!

We are in the people business.

We are the first of a new breed of organisation of whom you will undoubtedly see and hear more of as we progress into the 21st Century.

Our business is people and their behaviour. We can assist you to find and develop a highly motivated workforce. We can also assist you to maximise the effect of your advertising and the public front that you present to your potential consumers or end-users. Pure business psychology!

Mindworld-The total solution in people!

We can assist your business by searching for and selecting top quality people. We can also assess your current training needs and provide bespoke training to suit your exact requirements. Our unique and highly acclaimed audio business books will then provide an extra source of in-car training. We also have the specialist expertise of ensuring that your medium for reaching and influencing clients and customers, such as your design and advertising campaigns, are more effective!

- team building
- motivational leadership
- mastering change
- time management
- stress management
- neuro linguistic programming

- search and selection
- benchmarking
- keynote speakers
- graphic & website design
- advertising copy
- corporate entertainment

- visioneering
- psychology of design
- influence
- communication skills
- personal development & attitude
- sales

To find out more about our services there are five ways to contact us.

1. Phone us on 01377 257191.
2. Fax us on 01377 257191.
3. E-Mail us on SOLUTIONS@MINDWORLD.CO.UK
4. Contact us on our website at www.mindworld.co.uk
5. Write to us at Mindworld Ltd., P.O. Box 39, Driffield, YO25 9WH

Check out our audio business books - available from most good book shops via *Datum Marketing*. Quote the isbn number and they will order it for you.

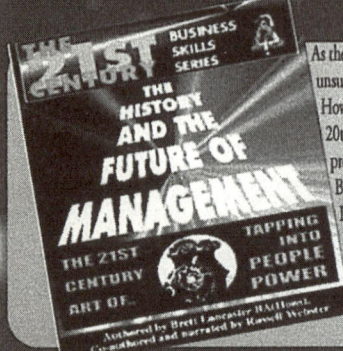

As the world hurtles into the new millennium, evolving and changing at an almost unsustainable pace, what skills and qualities must a 21st Century manager acquire and possess? How different will they be from a 20th. Century manager? What did business learn from the 20th Century management gurus? After 'excellence', 'chaos' and 'TQM' what are they predicting for the shape of tomorrow's manager? Which one's, if any, are right? What are Brett Lancaster and Russell Webster predicting for the future.

In this audio you will discover a unique fusion of thinking by these two established and respected specialists from different fields. One thing that is common to their thinking is that the main resource of the future is people. Learning how to manage the people resource, and bring the best out of them.

Title:-The History and the Future of Management Subtitle: The 21ST Century Art of Tapping into People Power! ISBN: 1-900165-22-8
Running Time : Approx 75 mins Price: £9.95 (including VAT) Author: Brett Lancaster BA (Hons) and Russell Webster Narrator: Russell Webster

In this audio you will be able to assess how much has changed in the world over a mere thirty years or so, and how much change you are likely to witness. The recent pace of both technological and sociological change has however brought its challenges for many people....With continued downsizing, greater output expectancy from fewer workers, increasing robotisation and computerisation and with life expectancy now over eighty and the pending economic crisis facing many countries, of having too few workers to fund pensions, a different approach to both work and social life will be needed to survive in the future. This audio will seriously make you stop and think about the way that you plan your future.

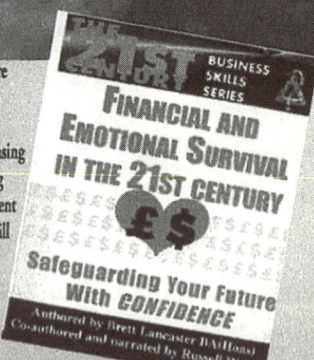

Title:-Financial and Emotional Survival in the 21ST Century Subtitle: Safeguarding your Future With Confidence! ISBN: 1-900165-23-6
Running Time : Approx 74 mins   Price: £9.95 (including VAT) Author: Brett Lancaster BA (Hons) and Russell Webster Narrator: Russell Webster

In this audio book you will learn how to make AIDA'S pussy P.U.R.R and truly maximise the effectiveness of all advertising copy that you write. Whether you are writing newspaper adverts, flyers, brochures, mailshot copy or targeted letters there are four specific steps highlighted that must be followed.

P stands for interrupting people's thought PATTERNS and creating their undivided attention. U stands for addressing and targeting someone's UNDERLYING MOTIVE to purchase your product or service. R stands for creating a REACTION TIMESCALE and a sense of urgency. R stands for providing a simple RESPONSE MECHANISM. Much of the information in this audio draws upon the principles of Neuro Linguistic Programming(NLP), which is considered to be at the cutting edge of human communication.

Companies and individuals who are already using the principles in this audio are achieving extraordinary results.

Title:-Stroking A.I.D.A.'S Pussy Subtitle: The 21ST Century Way to write highly successful adverts, brochures, mailshot copy and break up arguments! ISBN: 1-900165-24-4   Running Time : Approx 73 mins Publication Date: April 1998   Price: £9.95 (including Vat) Author Russell Webster

This revolutionary cassette pulls heavily upon NLP (Neuro Linguistic Programming) which is considered to be at the cutting edge of modern communication.

In a world that is changing rapidly so too are selling techniques. Old fashioned methods no longer apply and you need to develop new skills to prosper in the future. This tape will ensure that you can do just that! Discover: The Three Stages Of The Selling Process That You Must Master. How You Can Become A Great 'People-Person' And Enhance And Improve Your Sales Massively! How To Make A Powerful First Impression With Anyone You May Come Into Contact With. How To Create An Instant Rapport With People You Have Just Met!

How To Build Your Own Confidence. How To Become A Communication Expert. How To Gain Advance Information On Your Prospective Client To Hugely Increase Your Results. How Everyone Has A Different Mind Method And A Different Motivation Method; How To Use It To Write More Orders Than You Ever Dreamed Possible! The Questions That You Must Ask To Find Out Exactly Why Someone Will Buy From You. The Five Most Powerful Words In The World That Will Help You To Great Selling Success....... W..W..H..T..H.? The Power Of The Amazing Timeblind Question. How To Create A Never-Ending List Of Referrals. SUSS will help you to revitalise your selling and to realise your true potential for success.

Title:-SUSS. Subtitle: The 21st Century Way to Sell your Product, your Service, or Yourself!
ISBN: 1-900165-16-3   Running Time : 74 mins Publication Date: April 1998   Price: £9.95 (including VAT) Author and Narrator: Russell Webster

Why does one person seem totally at ease on a stage or whilst giving a presentation and another seem terrified? Is it because the FEAR OF PUBLIC SPEAKING is ranked as second in line to most people's greatest fear: FEAR OF LOSS, such as death. In this audio you will learn how to OVERCOME that FEAR. How to gain total control of an audience. How to speak with total confidence. How to keep your audience involved and how to round it all off with a guaranteed method of achieving a standing ovation.

CONFIDENCE
CONTROL
FEEDBACK
ASSERTIVENESS
APPLAUSE
OVATIONS

Title:- DOING IT STANDING UP Subtitle: The Ultimate Guide to Confident and Successful Public Speaking!
ISBN: 1-900165-25-2   Running Time : Approx 73 mins Publication Date: Sept 1998
Price: £9.95 (including VAT) Author and Narrator: Russell Webster

We also produce a range of 'lifeskills' titles-covering those areas that they simply did not teach you at school!

A recent survey has shown that 90% of all visits to the doctor are caused by or made worse by stress, depression, or other brain related illness. An unhappy, unhealthy and unfit brain can also lead to an unhappy, unhealthy and unfit body. Whereas a fit and healthy mind, or brain can promote a general sense of well-being that spreads throughout the whole body.
In this audio you will be able to carry out a quick 'check-up from the neck up' and assess your level of mental fitness and learn a few practical tips and tricks to boost your level of positive thinking. This is a pilot audio tape for a series of twenty six. A stands for Attitude. B stands for.....?

Title: The A to Z of Mental Fitness.
Subtitle: A Beginner's Guide To The Personal Benefits Of Positive Thinking ISBN: 1-900165-21-X
Running Time : 78 Mins Publication Date: April 1998 Price: £9.95 (including VAT) Author and Narrator: Russell Webster

Using the principles of NLP (Neuro Linguistic Programming) as well as superb music specially written to complement the spoken word, this ground-breaking double Audio Cassette will enable the listener to discover: Their true character and what makes them tick. What is truly important in their lives. The Critical importance of setting realistic goals. How to influence themselves and others. How certain human needs have to be fulfilled. How to put all of the secrets into action! What did Socrates say to the young man who sought wisdom? Why do so many rock and film stars hate their success? Why was Roger Bannister a trend-setter; breaking more than just the four-minute mile? What is a losers-limp? Why must you avoid the dreamstealers, the whingers, the gossips, the blamers, the moaners and the excuse-makers at all cost?

What do Michelangelo, Socrates and Colonel Saunders all have in common? What was Abraham Maslow's theory? What was Walt Disney's tip for success? What did they teach at Harvard that changed and enriched some people's lives massively? This entertaining and fascinating double audio will enable the listener to reach their true potential and find happiness and success!

Title:-7 Secrets Subtitle: The Guiding Principles of all Success and Happiness!
ISBN: 1-900165-19-8 Running Time: 107 mins Publication Date: April 1998
Price: £14.95 (including VAT) Author and Narrator: Russell Webster

There are millions of single people world-wide- 8 million in the UK alone- and This figure is growing daily. This tape is for everyone who is single... but who does not want to be! Find out:
Why everyone needs love and belonging? Where to find your soulmate? How do you attract a potential partner to you?
You will find the answer to these questions and many more in this highly acclaimed and very practical audio cassette. Discover where the game of love is played. Discover the secrets of attracting people to you. Discover how to create instant rapport and harmony. Discover what makes people fall in love and how to make them fall for you. Discover how to be a successful communicator - the NLP way. Discover how to be a great conversationalist. Discover where your Prince or Princess is waiting for you.

Title:-The Love Game
Subtitle: How to Find and Attract the Partner of your Dreams!
ISBN: 1-900165-17-1 Running Time : 73 mins
Publication Date: April 1998 Price: £9.95 (including VAT) Author and Narrator: Russell Webster

This award winning tape contains priceless information that will help you understand yourself better at the same time as gaining insights into how to bring your own children up to be happy and well balanced. Critical issues discussed include:

ABOUT YOU:
Discover why your childhood experiences affect you today. Discover which of the four 'life-positions' you have adopted: how and why you feel the way that you do about yourself and about others. Discover what your own personal Mindmethod is..........? Discover why you were 'terrible' at the age of two. Discover why you might experience mood swings. Discover how your health and even your lifespan may have been affected by your childhood.

ABOUT YOUR CHILD: Discover the greatest gift that you can give your child. Discover how the first hour of your child's life is probably the most important hour of all; how your newborn thinks, feels inside, and sees the world, in those first precious moments and how you can provide emotional stability for him or her. Discover how your child's brain develops and how you can provide a head start for your child socially and in their career. Discover how critically important breast-feeding is and how it can even effect your child's immune system. Discover why 'cot-death' does not occur in certain countries, and what you might learn from it. Discover the potential harm of using drugs to assist your child's birth. Discover why you should consider allowing your child to sleep in the same room with you. Discover all of this and much, much more.....

THE CRITICAL CHILDHOOD YEARS !
Why *you* Became The Way You Are Today And How To Make An Enormous Difference In The Life Of Your Child...

Authored and Narrated by Russell Webster & DR C.M.Viarisi MB.BS.MRCGP.DRCOG

Title:-The Critical Childhood Years Subtitle: Why you became the way you are today and how to make an enormous difference to the life of your child ISBN: 1-900165-18-X   Running Time : 80 Minutes Publication Date: April 1998

Also available on CD and cassette-

The first title in the TIMELINE SERIES
Combining music, the power of relaxation therapy, and many Neuro Linguistic Programming principles, author and composer Russell Webster introduces you to your own individual TIMELINE: YOUR LIFE PATH!
This journey into the past and into the future will empower YOU to build self-esteem and confidence, overcome fears and phobias and abandon limiting beliefs.
Those who have already listened to Choices describe this audio self-improvement programme as most effective", "deeply healing" and "state-of-the-art".

Title:CHOICES: Choose your own past and create YOUR OWN FUTURE! Running time : 78 mins
Publication Date: April 1998
Price: £13.95 (including VAT)
Author and Narrator: Russell Webster

Description: Peter Thomson explains how the awesome powers of your imagination, and visualisation can be employed to achieve your desired results. He also reinforces the importance of having a purpose in life, and how to discover that purpose by giving a step-by-step guide to setting goals to help achieve it.

ABOUT THE AUTHOR:
Peter Thomson is a highly successful businessman who is regarded as one of the UK's leading personal development strategists; with a number of best selling books, audio programmes and seminars to his credit.

Title: Tomorrow Today ISBN: 1-900165-015
Running Time : 78 mins Publication Date: April 1998   Price: £13.95 (including VAT)
Author and Narrator: Peter Thomson & Russell Webster

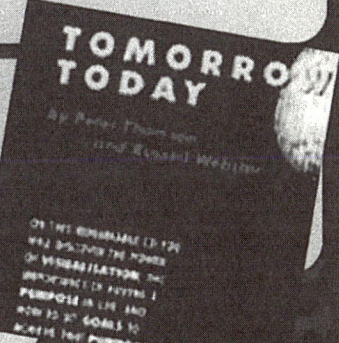

Disc 1: Choices - Choose your own path and create your own future! (Details as before)
Disc 2: Tomorrow Today - Visualise tomorrow's dreams and goals .. and start achieving them today! (Details as before)
Disc 3: A Journey in Time - Relax and enjoy your life on your timeline!
In this third CD of the set, Russell Webster explains the importance of aligning your values and beliefs with your goals before being able to set about any lasting success, thereafter it leads to a guided induction to your timeline, allowing you to `fly solo', and explore either your past or your future.
Disc 4: Innocence - From child to manchild and beyond to the brightest star in the sky The World's first rock music personal development concept album. It offers a fundamental understanding of why children develop and grow up with such a low sense of self-esteem and how others deal with their own low sense of worth by battering down the egos of others.

Title: Mind Explorations ISBN: 1-900165-090
Running Time : 78 mins Publication Date: April 1998 Price: £49.95 (including VAT)
Author and Narrator: Peter Thomson & Russell Webster
4-SET CD (including "CHOICES" and "TOMORROW TODAY")

Whether you are at the start of the evening or reaching the end of a long night this is the perfect album to wind down and relax to! The drumbeats, the percussion, the synthesiser sounds and the sparse vocals all blend and fuse together hypnotically allowing you to wind down, `chill out' and lose yourself in a fantasy world.

"In modern terms this is a classic chill-out album. If you like albums such as those from Enigma or those from Deep Forest or Sacred Spirit then you will love Seven Secrets by the Mindmaster."

Seven Secrets employs the use of modern dance beats tucked beneath an emotive pastiche of string sounds, percussion, analogue synthesiser effects and floating female vocals by Natalie.V, Jody Holmes, and Claire Eastwood..

"High above the plains, close to the hilltop, nestled into a warm, sheltered glade, that was protected by trees softly blowing in the mountain breeze, they settled down to relax and listen to the words of wisdom from he that knew. They drank from a specially prepared potion that readied their minds and........they listened. As each secret was revealed to them a light of understanding lit up inside them and was followed by a calm and tranquillity they had never known before."

Mindmaster CD
isbn 1-900165-20-1
£13.95 inc VAT

Contact us now for any of Mindworld's services or if you are unable to buy any of our products from your nearest bookshop.

Five ways to contact us.

1. Phone us on 01377 257191.
2. Fax us on 01377 257191.
3. E-Mail us on SOLUTIONS@MINDWORLD.CO.UK
4. Contact us via our website at WWW.MINDWORLD.CO.UK
5. Write to us at Mindworld Ltd., P.O. Box 39, Driffield, YO25 9WH

One small piece of information or knowledge could make a significant difference to all aspects of your life...

now